How to Start a Book Blog:
A Step by Step Guide

How to Start a Book Blog:
A Step by Step Guide

Rachel Carney

Published by Created to Read
2018

Cover image created by Huw Aaron

First Printing: 2018

ISBN 978-0-244-07196-7

Created to Read
www.createdtoread.com

Introduction

On 23rd January 2016 I decided to create a book blog. Nearly two months later my blog went live, and it has been an incredible journey since then. In fact it's been one gigantic learning curve. I received over 300 views on the very first day (which is pretty good for a new blog) and one year later I had reached a total of 10,000 views. At the time of writing, my blog is now receiving well over 1000 views per month. Take a look – the address is **https://createdtoread.com**.

I had never even looked at a book blog before I started, although I knew that they existed, and had stumbled across them occasionally by accident on my travels across the web. I had no expertise, no blogging knowledge, and very little money, but I did have the most important element that you need when setting up a blog – time, and plenty of it.

I began by trawling the internet in search of advice. There's a lot of advice out there about how to create a blog, much of which is extremely helpful. But there was hardly anything aimed at the very specific sphere of 'book blogs', so here it is: a book designed especially for anyone wanting to set up a book blog.

This book is also aimed at writers who would like to create their own website, reaching out to new audiences and providing a platform for their work. Book blogs are the perfect base from which to promote and sell your own books.

Note: There are links within this book which will direct you to various websites and blogs. There is also very specific information about social media. Due to the fast-changing nature of the online world, it is possible that these links and details may change.

Contents

Chapter 1: Which Kind of Book Blog?

There are thousands of blogs out there. Think of a subject, and you'll find a blog on it. Essentially, it's a diary, available for anyone to see. It can be a simple blog by itself, or it can be a small part of a much larger website. It can be run by one person from their own home, or several people, or a business.

But the **book blog** is something else. It is an essential (though unofficial) part of the global publishing industry. Self-published authors often rely heavily on book bloggers and blog tours to reach out to readers and boost sales, and authors published via traditional routes often benefit from them too.

The term **book blog** can be used to cover a wide range of websites which all have one thing in common – they're created by people who love reading, and their focus is books. But there are different styles and purposes, and I have split them into five separate types:

Type 1 - The Author's Blog

Many authors soon discover that they need to put some effort into marketing their own books online. Whether they have gone through the traditional publishing route, or have attempted to make their way through self-publishing, there is much to be said for a good quality author's website which will promote their work to a wide audience.

Here are some examples of author's websites which include an interesting blog –

Shannon Selin – a writer of historical fiction

https://shannonselin.com/

Christina Thatcher – a poet

https://christinathatcher.com/

Roy Marshall – a poet

https://roymarshall.wordpress.com/

Sarah J. Palmer – a fiction writer

https://confessionsofalitaddict.wordpress.com/

One of the things that search engines particularly like is a website where new content is posted on a regular basis, and blogs are an easy way to create new content without too much effort. Readers also like this, as it adds something special, and gives them an incentive to keep going back for more.

Examples of typical author's blog posts might include:

- Inspiration – what inspired you to write your book
- Work in progress – what you're working on at the moment
- Currently reading – this could be a review of a book you're reading or one you've just read

- Journal posts – a few hundred words about your work as a writer e.g. attending a book signing or researching a scene for your next book
- Interviews with fellow authors – this will add a bit of interest and you might get a link back from their website to your own

Type 2 - The Basic Book Review Blog

There are thousands of book blogs which follow the simple format of posting short book reviews, often providing a rating for the book (e.g. 5 Stars). Many of these cover a variety of genres, and some post several times a week. Most are run by just one person, whilst others involve a whole team of reviewers, enabling them to cover more ground.

Here are a couple of examples, both of which have multiple contributors:

https://rosieamber.wordpress.com/

http://readingforsanity.blogspot.co.uk/

Type 3 - The Themed Book Review Blog

This is a format which I think works particularly well – a book blog which follows a particular theme or genre. Whilst I read quite a wide variety of genres, there are many readers out there for whom fantasy or historical fiction is their genre of choice. They are far more likely to visit a book blog on that particular theme, than to visit a generic book blog which covers multiple genres.

The theme doesn't necessarily need to be a specific genre. I've seen some great book blogs which have interesting and quirky themes, such as:

- Books in translation
- A challenge e.g. to read 50 books in a year

Here are two examples:

http://readdiversebooks.com/ - A blog with a focus on books written by people from a range of ethnic and racial backgrounds other than white Europeans.

http://dearauthor.com/ - A blog which contains reviews written in the form of a letter to the author.

Type 4 - The Book Blog PLUS EXTRAS

This is a bit more unusual, and can take a variety of forms. It is a blog which will branch out into other areas more often covered by traditional magazines. In fact, there is a fine line between an online magazine and this kind of book blog.

As well as book reviews, they may also include reviews of events, interviews, features, news items and sometimes creative writing e.g. poems or short stories written by the blogger themselves or by others who submit their work.

Type 5 - The Display Blog

Journalism students are often encouraged to create their own blog, sometimes as part of an assignment. The blog acts primarily as a way of showcasing their writing skills, so that any potential employers, editors or publishers can see examples of their work.

They will often include links to any published work that has appeared online – a kind of online writing CV. A blog is also useful for getting their name out there into the world of journalism – in a similar way to an author's blog. It helps them to practise their writing too, on a regular basis.

My Own Blog

My blog is a bit of a mix, with book reviews, author interviews and features, as well as reviews of festivals and events. In this way, it is similar to an online magazine, but the majority of posts are book reviews.

There are three main themes:

- The book reviews cover a range of genres, but there is a strong emphasis on my favourites (poetry, historical fiction and literary fiction)
- I often focus on the work of Welsh writers (as I live in Wales)
- There's an emphasis on literary festivals and events. I felt that this would make my blog stand out from other blogs, and I really enjoy attending literary festivals

Take Your Pick…

There is no set way of creating a book blog. You can follow one of these formats, or copy the style of a blog you like, or do something entirely different. But it is useful to work out early on what kind of blog you want to end up with, so that you can set up a structure that works well for that format.

It is crucial to choose a theme that you have a real interest in – something you enjoy talking about.

- Take a look at your bookshelves for ideas.

- Write a list of the books you've read recently, and another list of the books you'd like to read.

- Think about the different types of book blog, and what you want to achieve by creating your own blog.

- Do you enjoy reading books that are really unusual? Or do you have a passion for fantasy or crime fiction? Or perhaps you'd like to set yourself a challenge?

It's worth spending some time thinking about this. Once you've started to get some ideas, you're ready to move on to the research stage.

Chapter 2: The Research Stage

Step 1) Research Existing Book Blogs

It's important to spend time on research, to get an idea of what you like and what you don't like. Start making a list of ideas, and save a list of links to your favourite blogs, so you can keep going back and reminding yourself how they do it. A good place to start is **http://bookbloggerlist.com/** where you can see a wide range of styles and search by genre.

Here's an example of what you might include in your list:

Things I like

- Easy to read
- A simple name
- Each book rated out of 10
- A menu across the top so you can select your favourite genre
- A link to their Twitter feed on the homepage
- Not just book reviews – special features and author interviews

Things I don't like

- Coloured text on a black background
- Lots of adverts
- Very long paragraphs

- Lots of background images
- A font that's difficult to read

Step 2) Pick Your USP

Once you've done a fair amount of research, it's time to pick your USP (unique selling point) – to decide what your blog will offer that other blogs don't. If you're just doing it for fun, this doesn't matter so much, but if you want to get lots of views, comments and subscribers, then it's essential not to just copy other blogs. I picked a few USPs for mine, partly because I couldn't decide between them, but it's also helpful to cover a bit of ground, as it widens your appeal.

My main USP is a strong focus on literary events and festivals, because I wanted the blog to offer insights and details that wouldn't be available anywhere else, and I enjoy attending literary events. I haven't seen any other book blogs which do this in the same way, so that makes it stand out.

You may choose a USP which is more quirky or unusual… perhaps an interesting way of reviewing the books you read, or a unique rating system.

Step 3) Think About Your Audience

It's important to think about who will read your blog. Do you want your blog to appeal to people who read for a hobby, academics or students? I try to write in a clear and accessible way that will be engaging for people who haven't studied English literature, but not too boring and simplistic for those that have. I try to use an informal tone of voice, and I avoid using terminology that people won't recognise. If I do refer to something that people may not be familiar with, I try to explain it or link to a website which provides an explanation.

You also need to think about why people read blogs. Blog readers often want to read a post that's useful, not just entertaining. This is something that I really struggled with when I first started. I just wanted to write about books, but I couldn't really see how this would be helpful to anyone. I've learnt now that there are ways of approaching all sorts of topics so that people will find the post useful.

For example, a book review may help someone to decide whether or not to read or buy the book, and a review of a festival may help someone decide whether to attend it next year, and can also provide snippets of interesting details about the work of writers they may not have come across before.

It's particularly useful to provide links to other websites. One of my most popular posts has been a list of literary festivals in Wales, which contains links to the websites for those festivals, and other link posts have also been popular. See Chapter 5 for more advice about listings.

Step 4) Create A Name

You'll need to create a unique name for your blog. The best way to do this is to write down as many key words relating to your topic as possible, and rearrange them in all sorts of ways, then type them into a search engine and cross them off your list if blogs with that name already exist. This will take time, and it's important to search thoroughly, to make sure you don't replicate an existing blog name.

Try using more than one search engine, and don't just look at the first page of results.

You could use your own name in the title, e.g. 'Rob's Book Review Blog' or 'Rebecca Simkins Reviews'. Once you've found something, ask friends and family what they think, then try typing it into Twitter and Facebook as well, to check whether the name is available there.

Here is an example list to get you started:

- Read / Reading
- Book / Books
- Review / Reviews
- Blog
- Novel / Novels
- Fiction

It's also worth remembering that blogs can have a global audience. People all over the world will be able to see your blog. One of my original ideas for a blog name was 'Read in the Diff', as the local name for Cardiff is 'the Diff'. But I realised fairly soon (after asking family members what they thought) that most people would not know what this means.

Step 5) Find A Hosting Site

All websites need to be stored somewhere, and that is usually on a hosting site. It's more secure than hosting it yourself. Basically, there are two main options for hosting your blog:

Option 1 – The Free Blog

You can create a blog very easily for free, using something like WordPress.com or Blogspot.com. This is the simplest option, as you don't need to worry about payment or security, and you will be able to set up the blog straight away. The downside is that you will have less control over it, the hosting company has the right to place adverts on your site, and you will have something like 'WordPress' or 'Blogspot' in the domain name (web address) which makes it long, wieldy and less memorable.

Option 2 – The Blog That Costs Money

You can pay to have your own domain name e.g. **www.createdtoread.com** and to have the blog hosted for you. There are hundreds of hosting sites out there, and a minefield of comparison websites and varied costs (from around $3-$5 per month at the cheaper end).

It's almost impossible to find advice which is completely honest and neutral, as the hosting sites pay people to promote them with positive reviews. But eventually you just have to make a decision based on how big your budget is, and what kind of website you want to create.

Things to consider:

How much you're prepared to pay. My hosting site stated monthly costs, but expected you to pay most of this up front. There was also a separate payment for renewing the domain name each year.

Whether to purchase hosting for a year or a longer period of time. At the end of that time, they may try to increase their prices, so you might need to change hosting sites which can be a complex and time-consuming process. I purchased a three-year package.

Whether there are additional costs e.g. to register a domain name or get security packages. Security is important.

Loading speed (the length of time it takes for webpages to load) and **uptime** (how much time your website is likely to be live and available for people to view, as opposed to temporarily not working).

The size of your blog. The average blog won't get more than 10,000 views per month so you can probably go for a cheaper, smaller option unless you anticipate any of the following: becoming extremely popular very quickly, including lots of film clips and large images on your blog, or developing a complex website. It's incredibly difficult to estimate the size of your blog before you've even created it yet, but most simple blogs will not take up much space.

Customer service. Some hosting sites offer customer support 24/7, whilst others may be based on the other side of the globe, and more limited in their support. Be careful to avoid hosts that only offer support during their daytime / your night.

Email address. Some hosting packages come with an email address, so you can have a separate email to your personal one e.g. sam@samsbookblog.com. It helps to create an extra layer of privacy between your private world and your online presence. It also looks professional. You can always set up an automatic redirect so that you don't miss any emails.

Security and back-up. Check whether these are included in the price. Having a regular back-up for your blog is essential, as things can easily go wrong. My hosting package included free daily back-ups.

I went with SiteGround in the end, because it wasn't too expensive, they use WordPress, which is fairly straightforward and easy for beginners, and they seemed to have more positive than negative reviews. It's been ok so far. And they haven't paid me anything to say this!

Here are a couple of comparison websites that you may find helpful:

https://hostingfacts.com/

https://hostadvice.com/hosting-companies/

Chapter 3: The Planning Stage

Step 1) Pick Your 'Theme'

Once you've purchased your hosting package or created your free site, you'll have a domain name which is your very own unique name – effectively the title of your blog. This is the time to pick a 'theme' (website design). There are hundreds of free themes available, and you could literally spend days looking through them. You can also purchase a theme, or pay to have one designed for you, but I decided to go for a free one. It took me a while to find one that I liked.

You'll have to think about the general look of your blog, whether you need space for a logo and menu, what kind of colours you like, and the layout. A couple of things that I really wanted for my blog were a typical website layout with a dropdown menu along the top, and a clear place for people to subscribe (RSS feed). I also wanted the text to be in a sans serif font, so it would be easy to read.

You might want to choose a theme which allows space to add more in the future, such as widgets for social media. It's also essential to pick a theme which is mobile friendly, so your blog will be visible on phones, tablets and other devices. I would recommend spending a few days looking at different themes (if you're using WordPress, just type 'free WordPress themes' into a search engine).

Narrow it down to four or five, download one of them, and then begin to create some posts and pages, adding images and links. Once you've got some draft content (it doesn't have to be finished) it will be much easier to see how the blog will look. You can easily change the theme at this early stage. If you change the theme later on it can sometimes cause problems with pre-existing content, so it's better to spend time making sure you get it right at the beginning.

It's useful to consider at this stage how images will display on your blog. Most themes limit the options available for displaying images in different ways. With my theme, I can display them as a square thumbnail, a medium sized landscape image or a full-sized landscape image. There isn't much room for variation. I decided this would work well for my blog, but you may want more control over your images.

Adding Extras: Widgets & Plug-Ins

It's worth bearing in mind that you can always add extra functions to your blog in the form of widgets or plug-ins.

Widgets

These come as part of the theme you pick and they are all optional. They often appear down the side of your homepage, and will stay in place no matter which page or post you are looking at. They can include:

- live feeds from social media channels e.g. Twitter
- a list of categories or recent posts
- an RSS feed (allowing viewers to subscribe to your blog)
- space to add adverts in future
- a search box

Plug-ins

Plug-ins are additional to your site (they literally 'plug in'), and can be used for all sorts of purposes...

- to create a pop-up window
- to create a ranking system for books
- to set up a poll for people to cast votes
- to create metadata (see page 37 for more information)

If you want your blog to do something that you've seen happening on other websites, and there's no way to do it within your theme, then search for a plug-in and see if you can find one that will help.

Some plug-ins cost money but there are plenty of free ones. Check that the plug-in is compatible with your version of WordPress, or whatever you are using, and update it each time a new version becomes available. You can turn them on or off, if you change your mind.

Step 2) Plan Your Structure

It's useful at this stage to start thinking about what kind of content you will want on your blog, and how this will be displayed. My advice would be to draw out your ideal structure on a piece of paper. You may not include everything to begin with, but it's useful to have an idea of what you're aiming for. Most blogs have a very simple structure. Mine is a little more complicated than most. There are three things to focus on when considering your blog's structure – the **pages**, the **posts** and the **categories**.

Pages

A page is static and if someone signs up to follow your blog, they won't be notified when you publish new pages. Pages are useful for the more boring (but necessary) pieces of information. Most blogs have an **About** page, and some have a **Reviewing Policy** page, whilst others also have a **Privacy Policy** page and a **Contact** page.

Posts

Every time you create a new post, the people who follow your blog will receive an email. The most recent post will usually appear at the top of the list, with older posts moving down as new ones appear. Posts tend to be book reviews, but could also be features, interviews or something else.

Categories

Categories are used to create structure for your posts. If you want, you can just leave your posts in a straightforward list (which is common for book blogs, and some themes are set up this way) but you also have the option to divide them into categories e.g. by genre. This will help viewers to find the posts that are of most interest to them. You can have 'parent' and 'child' categories, where one is a sub-category of the other.

Example 1 – Pages In A Menu

Take a look at the following image, which shows a screenshot of the menu on my blog's homepage. You can see that I've selected the **About** tab. **About** is a page, and so are the other things listed in this drop-down menu. Each page is constructed in the same way. The **About** page is the parent page, with the child pages appearing underneath.

Example 2 – Categories In A Menu

Imagine that I am starting my blog from scratch, and have decided to create my very first blog post. When I create the post, there are several things I need to do, including giving it a title. But I also need to select which categories I want it to appear in. On my blog, all my book reviews go in the **Book Reviews** category. This means that if someone clicks on **Book Reviews** they will see all the book review posts. But I usually select a genre as well, e.g. **Historical Fiction**. This means that someone could click on the **Historical Fiction** category and this post will appear in the list.

You can add categories at a later date, move them around, change their names or even remove them altogether. So don't worry if you change your mind. However, it's useful to spend some time working out what the structure might look like overall, and how posts will connect with each other. I often write posts which fit into more than one category, and that's fine.

The next image is a screenshot of the 'Menu Structure' in my WordPress Dashboard, where you can see how both pages and categories can be included in the menu. **About** and **Book Reviews** are both aligned to the left, with other pages and categories indented and described as 'sub-items'.

Menu Structure

Drag each item into the order you prefer. Click the arrow on the right of the item to re

About	Page ▾
Contact *sub item*	Page ▾
Reviewing Policy *sub item*	Page ▾
Privacy Policy *sub item*	Page ▾
Book Reviews	Category ▾
Historical Fiction *sub item*	Category ▾
Poetry *sub item*	Category ▾
Crime/Thriller *sub item*	Category ▾

Step 3) Create A Brand

You're already half way there with a domain name – which is effectively your brand. An image or logo really helps. I was very lucky to have a friend who designed a logo for me.

It's best to keep a logo as simple as possible but also unique. It's important that you have space in your theme for it to appear. I spent a long time trying to find a theme which would allow space for a logo, and then asked my friend to design a logo which fitted in the space available, and matched the colours. I also used it as my logo on Twitter and Facebook, and on some business cards, and it's now on the front of this book!

But to make a brand work really well you also need consistency. Think about creating a certain 'look' to your blog posts and try to be consistent in how you use punctuation e.g. when referring to the title of a book I always type it in bold, but you could use speech marks or italics. Try to be consistent in how you use images, captions, paragraphs and links. This doesn't mean you can't do something different every once in a while, but it will help to create your brand.

Step 4) Create Social Media Accounts

Bloggers use social media as a way to encourage as many people as possible to visit their blog. There are many social media options, and social media is constantly changing. The trick is not to try and do everything at once. If social media is new to you I would recommend choosing just one platform (Twitter is the easiest option for a beginner) and then you won't feel too overwhelmed.

Twitter is a good place to connect with people you don't already know – writers, publishers and other book bloggers.

Facebook is better for connecting with your existing friends and it can be more difficult (in my experience) to quickly establish a big following, but it is worth persevering.

I use **Facebook**, **Twitter** and **Hootsuite**, but **Instagram** is another popular platform for book bloggers, and there are other social media platforms you could try.

Twitter

It's easy to set up a new Twitter account, but worth spending some time seeing how it works before you start tweeting. I would recommend setting up an account using your own name, as you can always change the handle (e.g. **@createdtoread**) at a later date.

You could also create an account where the name and the handle of your account are the same, but I prefer to have both my own full name and my blog name clearly visible, so people can search for me easily if they know either. Try to create a handle that is fairly short, as it takes up valuable characters, and this can make a difference in whether people interact with you or not.

Tweets	Following	Followers	Likes
2,580	2,818	1,755	2,433

Rachel Carney
@CreatedtoRead

Bookish, poetic, honorary Cardiffian, book blogger- createdtoread.com #BookReview #amreading #litfests #amwriting

Cardiff, Wales

createdtoread.com

Tweets   Tweets & replies   Media

Pinned Tweet

Rachel Carney @CreatedtoRead · Aug 11
Adding more #creativewriting groups in #(blog - createdtoread.com/creative-writi...
#amwriting #amreading #Wales

It's also worth spending some time getting just the right image for your cover photo (across the top) and logo (in the circle), and creating a relevant and interesting profile, including a direct link to your blog. Type 'Twitter cover photo size' into a search engine and try to make sure yours fits. I use Microsoft Picture Manager (2010) to crop and re-size images, but there are plenty of other programmes you could use.

The challenge with Twitter is to get your message across in 280 characters or less. It's something you will soon get used to. Spend time reading other people's tweets and this will give you an idea of how it can work. Remember to include a link to your blog when you tweet.

Hashtags

Hashtags are a useful way of reaching out to a wider audience, especially early on, when you don't have many followers. They act as clickable links, so that if you click on **#BookReview** for example, you will be able to see all the tweets where people have used this particular phrase.

Try typing the following hashtags into a search engine:

#BookReview

#TuesdayBookBlog

#FolkloreThursday

#amreading

The first result will probably be a link to Twitter. Click on it and you'll see a menu along the top. 'Latest' is the most useful tab to look at, as it will show you the most recent tweets which have used this hashtag.

Spend some time on Twitter typing in words related to books with a # in front, and create a list of potential hashtags, then you can try them out and you'll soon see which ones are the most effective. Every now and then you'll see something topical trending such as **#WorldBookDay** or **#NationalPoetryDay** and it's worth making use of these opportunities.

You can try and create your own hashtag, but this is unlikely to be very effective unless you have something exceptionally interesting to tweet about, or a team of other Twitter users also planning to use the same hashtag. I've created a hashtag for a particular event before (**#EdwardThomas100**). It worked on a small scale, because there were a few other people who were also keen to use it.

Twitter Etiquette

There is a certain Twitter etiquette which is useful to learn. For example, if someone retweets your tweet, have a look on their profile and see if there's anything you can retweet in return. I don't do this very often, but I should do it more.

It's also worth using the 'pinned tweet' option, which allows you to select one tweet to stay at the top of your profile. I change my pinned tweet every few weeks, sometimes more often. I try to pick one which contains a direct link to my blog and an interesting image, which has been retweeted and liked a few times.

Don't bombard people with tweets. It's a good idea to tweet at least once a day, but don't retweet too much (perhaps no more than 15 times a day). If you're going to tweet a lot then make sure you vary it – don't just copy and paste the same text. People will soon get fed up and unfollow you. It's better not to tweet than to tweet something really boring or repeat yourself too often. Look at the following examples, where I've advertised the same book review using different text.

Tweet 1

"Her language is fresh, raw and earthy, with a strong ecological message" http://createdtoread.com/poetry-review-slant-light-sarah-westcott #Poetry review #TuesdayBookBlog #amreading

Tweet 2

"a slim-lined #poetry collection which hides a wealth of natural wonder" Review of Slant Light by @sarahwestcott1 http://createdtoread.com/poetry-review-slant-light-sarah-westcott

Quotes and images go down well on Twitter, and if you're tweeting about a book review then it's worth mentioning the author and publisher directly (e.g. @SerenBooks), as they're likely to retweet it if they appreciate the review!

One of my most successful tweets was popular because the author really liked the review, and she had a very large following on Twitter.

Once you've set up your Twitter account, try to spend a few minutes every day following other book bloggers, publishers and writers. As you begin to tweet interesting content, you'll soon find that people start following you back. But don't watch the numbers too closely – they will go down as well as up.

It's also important to remember that all sorts of people use Twitter. Some of them will be sensitive, and some will be rude or annoying. Remember that you're interacting with real people (it is easy to forget this sometimes!) and be polite. If someone interacts with you, it's a good idea to respond. You can block people if they are causing trouble.

Useful Twitter Rules to Bear in Mind

If you begin a tweet with a direct mention (e.g. @JonnyAuthor) then only that person can see your tweet, along with anyone else who follows both you and @JonnyAuthor.

If you want to respond to someone but you want everyone to be able to see the message, try placing a full stop at the beginning, or mentioning their Twitter handle later on in the tweet.

Direct messages can be really useful as a way of making contact with authors or publishers in a more private way. I have met several people through Twitter. However, you will only be able to use the direct message function if you follow each other. If you follow @JonnyAuthor but he doesn't follow you back, then you won't be able to send him a direct message. If you still want to contact him directly and don't mind other people being able to see your message, then you could tweet him with a mention e.g.

@JonnyAuthor I really liked your latest book – Would you be interested in an interview for my blog?

The likelihood is that if @JonnyAuthor is interested, then he'll follow you back and start a private conversation using direct messages.

Tools for Tracking Twitter

There are tools which you can use for various things such as checking who has followed you back, and unfollowing anyone who doesn't follow you back. There are also tools for creating an automatic direct message to be sent to anyone who follows you, which bloggers often use to promote their blog. However, I find these two things incredibly irritating, and so do many other people. Personally, I would not recommend using them.

Facebook

Many businesses, blogs and magazines have a Facebook Page. It's fairly simple to set up, but you do need your own Facebook account to do this. It's taking me a while to establish my Facebook page, but I often find that I get more blog views from Facebook than Twitter.

You'll need to come up with a description, and add your logo and a cover photo. Type 'correct size for a Facebook page cover image' into a search engine and you'll find the information you need to get the size and shape of your image right (this changes every now and then). I would advise playing about with this for a while before you decide on something. My Facebook page and Twitter profile have the same cover image, to help with brand consistency.

I usually advertise blog posts on Facebook by scheduling a message in advance, with one good image (more than one doesn't look as good), so that it appears on my blog's Facebook page. I then 'share' the post a few hours later, or the following day, on my own personal profile, so that people can click on a direct link either to my blog or to the page.

Hootsuite

There are various social media platforms which allow you to schedule messages in advance, and manage several social media accounts (e.g. Twitter and Facebook) from one place. I use Hootsuite because it was recommended to me. It's easy to set up an account, but you'll need to remember the passwords of any accounts you want to add.

I tend to schedule a blog post in advance (e.g. for 7am on a Tuesday), then I create a few tweets and a Facebook post, making sure they are scheduled for after the blog post goes live. This is crucial, as the permalink (e.g. **http://createdtoread.com/the-muse-jessie-burton/**) won't work until the post is live. I always check that my blog posts have gone live, just in case. On one occasion, I discovered a problem, so I was able to postpone all my pre-scheduled tweets until after I'd sorted out the issue (which turned out to be a computer error on my hosting site caused by the clocks going forward an hour for British Summer Time).

It is easy to schedule one message simultaneously for Facebook, Twitter and any other social media platforms, but I usually tailor the message slightly differently for each one.

Facebook messages work better with just one image, but you can include much more text, whereas there is less space for text on Twitter, and you can mention authors or publishers directly. Take a look at the following links to the same blog post. The first one was posted on Facebook and the second one on Twitter.

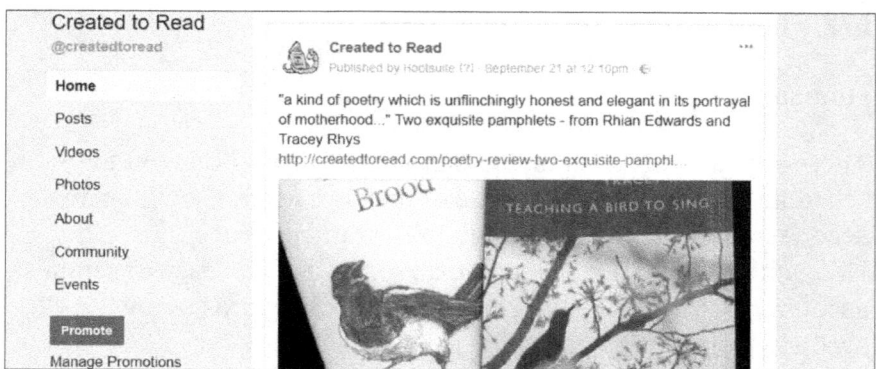

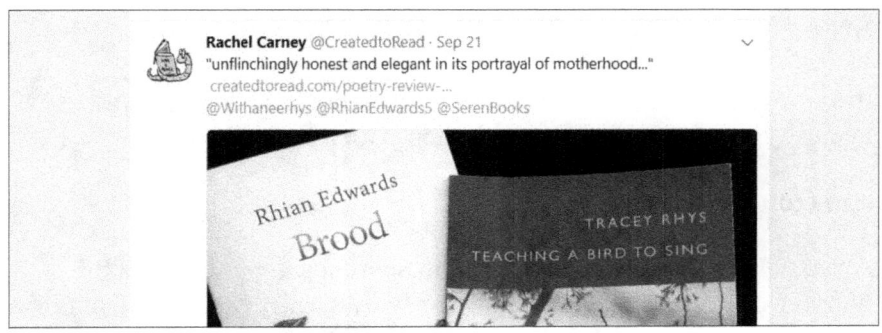

You can tweet or create Facebook posts to coincide with effective time windows. I often schedule my tweets for lunch time, as this catches people on their lunch break in the UK (where I'm based) and it also catches people getting up on the other side of the world (e.g. in the US). Play around with different times. It's also worth bearing in mind that many businesses will not monitor their social media accounts out of office hours.

When advertising a new blog post, I usually schedule one Facebook post and two or three tweets on the day it goes live. But I often schedule some more, similar tweets for a week or so later, and there's nothing wrong with alerting your followers to old blog posts from a few months ago, as they may well have missed reading the original post.

Twitter currently allows you to retweet each of your own tweets once, which can be helpful. But try not to do this too soon or too often. It's best to space out your tweets if they are similar or identical, otherwise you may lose followers.

Step 5) Amazon and Goodreads

It's important to know what else is out there, and how people use it, even if you never use these websites yourself.

Amazon

Amazon rates books more highly in searches depending on the number of reviews. Even negative reviews, or reviews of just a few words, can be useful for Amazon ratings. Many book bloggers post their reviews on Amazon as well as on their own blogs. This can be time consuming, but authors really appreciate it, especially if they've self-published or if they're with a small, independent publisher. It's entirely up to you whether you use Amazon or not.

My recommendation would be to post something on Amazon if you have the time, but keep it fairly short and simple, and different to the content of your blog post. Unfortunately, Amazon doesn't like it if you include direct links in your reviews, but you could mention your blog by name, so if people are interested they can search for it.

Goodreads

Goodreads is incredibly popular with readers, acting as both a social network and a place to promote books. It's particularly useful for authors, as you can create an 'author profile', add your books to lists, organise 'giveaways' and interact with readers, and there is even an option for linking with your blog.

If you are an author, the best way to set this up is to register for a Goodreads account, then search for one of your books using the ISBN. Once you've found your book, scroll down to the bottom and click on 'Is this you?' where you can submit your own details and apply for an author profile. There is plenty of advice online, specifically for authors, about how to make effective use of Goodreads.

If you haven't yet published any books, Goodreads can still be a useful place to interact with readers, post reviews and join groups. The best way to understand how it works is to register for an account and start exploring. Begin by rating books you've read and having a look at other people's profiles.

Chapter 4: Preparation & SEO

Once you've done the hard work of finding a hosting site, picking a theme and setting up social networking accounts, it's time to start thinking about producing some content for your blog. The following chapter deals with the nitty gritty of creating a content plan, planning a launch and search engine optimisation. Chapter 5 will provide advice on how to develop pages and blog posts.

Step 1) Decide How Often You Will Post

This is a difficult one. You have to bear in mind that the more often you post, the more views you will get on your blog. But you also don't want to stretch your content too far. If you only have time to write one good post each week, then by trying to write two or three a week you'll end up with poor quality posts that are rushed and boring. You also have to consider that if someone subscribes to your blog, they'll receive an email each time you post something, so you want it to be of good quality and worth clicking on the link.

Most bloggers suggest that regularity is the most important thing. Whether you decide to post once a day, twice a week, once a week, or once a month, the important thing is to stick to it regularly, but not to get too stressed if you miss one. No-one will notice the odd change to your routine every now and then.

You should also try and stick to a pattern e.g. posting every Tuesday. This could be because you have a day off on a Tuesday, or it could be that you're making use of regular hashtags on Twitter, such as:

#TuesdayBookBlog

#FridayReads

#FolkloreThursday

#SundayBlogShare

It's important to research hashtags before using them though, as they're not always what you might think.

I tend to schedule my blog posts for 7am in the morning, to fit in with my routine. I am usually able to spend a few minutes checking that the post has definitely gone live, and that it looks OK and the pictures are all correctly displayed.

Step 2) Plan Your Launch

You don't have to launch your blog, you can just add to it bit by bit and reveal it gradually to the world. But I wanted to create something which already had a decent amount of content, before I told people about it, so that it would look established and interesting.

As soon as you have a domain name, your blog exists for people to see online, whether you have added anything to it or not. But you don't really need to worry about this yet, as no search engines will have discovered it, and no-one will find it unless you give them the web address. I decided to download a plug-in which created a temporary holding page, so that whilst I was working on the blog, people could visit it and subscribe in advance. It also meant I could start creating the content and letting people know about it, but they wouldn't see it until I decided it was ready.

If you're going to do a launch, then you need to prepare some content in advance (I had several posts already live when I launched my blog). You'll need to pick a day to launch it, and you'll need to decide how you're going to tell people about it.

The best way of telling people about your blog is through social media, focusing initially on family and friends, but you could do what I did, and send out an email using MailChimp. It's free to create an account, but you'll need a list of email addresses. I spent a long time compiling contact lists using Excel (e.g. local writers, magazines and publishers), and sent an email announcing the launch of the blog. This was useful, to gain some interest on that first day, but the majority of my contacts have been built up slowly since then, using Twitter to connect with local arts organisations and publishers, and Facebook to connect with friends.

Other launch options might include:

- Writing a press release and sending it to media organisations (this works best if you have an interesting story to tell)

- Organising a 'giveaway' (giving out one or more copies of a book for free) or a competition with a good quality prize

- Organising a launch party, and inviting local writers, publishers and journalists (this would work best if you involved others in the event, e.g. a joint launch event with a local author publishing their debut novel)

Step 3) Create A Content Plan

Once you have a launch date in mind, it's best to create a calendar of what you'll write and when. I actually planned out two months' worth of posts in an Excel spreadsheet, and started writing them straight away. The more you write, the more you will get a feel for your own style. You can always go back and edit old posts if you change your mind.

Step 4) Include An RSS Feed

An RSS feed is a kind of form which appears on most blogs for people to type in their email address, to subscribe. They will then receive an email every time you write a new post. You don't need to include this feature, but gaining more subscribers can help increase the popularity of your blog. If you want to prove that your blog is successful, stating that you have a large number of subscribers can help publishers to see that it will be beneficial to give you free copies of their book in return for a review.

Your theme may already include an RSS feed, or you may need to add one using a plug-in or widget. Some blogs include a pop-up which appears whenever someone new arrives on the website, encouraging them to sign up. Pop-ups can be extremely irritating, but they can be a very effective way of getting people to sign up. Then they will be much more likely to visit your blog again.

If you do have an RSS feed, then you may want to ensure that you use the 'read more' feature on your blog, so that when people receive the email announcing that a new post has been added, they will only be able to see the first paragraph, and will need to click on a link to actually visit your blog in order to read the whole post. This is much better for your blog statistics.

Step 5) Search Engine Optimisation

Search Engine Optimisation (SEO) is about people being able to find your blog easily through search engines such as Google or Bing. When you initially make your blog live, it's highly unlikely that anyone will be able to find it using a search engine. There are various ways to improve your SEO. If this is something you care about, then I would suggest spending some time on it. You'll need to be patient though. It took about six months before I began to see a significant increase in search engine referrals.

To find out if your blog is definitely visible to search engines, wait a few weeks, until you have some posts or pages, giving the search engines time to find your site, and then copy a couple of sentences that seem unique and paste them directly into a search engine. If your blog doesn't appear, try it again with a different or longer piece of text, or a different search engine. If it still doesn't appear, then you know there is something wrong, and it's worth searching for advice online.

Potential problems that could prevent search engines from finding your blog:

- Too much Flash animation
- Not enough content containing relevant key words
- You may need to wait a bit longer or add some more posts

Here are a few suggestions for increasing your SEO, which seem to have worked for my blog, although I have no way of finding out which methods were the most effective:

Metadata

Metadata is the hidden data behind a webpage. It exists in code form (HTML) and helps search engines to find what they're looking for. Your blog will have metadata whether you put it there or not, so you may as well make it work as effectively as you can. If you're really keen, you can learn about how to do this yourself, but I opted for a free plug-in which works with my WordPress site (it's called 'Add Meta Tags').

It creates a set of metadata for the website as a whole and for each new blog post and page, highlighting key words. For example, if I write a book review of The Muse by Jessie Burton, I will ensure that 'Muse', 'Jessie' and 'Burton' as well as 'book' and 'review' appear in the metadata, so that if someone types something like "Review of The Muse by Jessie Burton" into a search engine, then my blog post will be listed in the results.

Structure - Tags & Categories

It can be helpful to imagine your blog in the form of a spider's web. The more links and internal connections it has, the easier it is for web crawlers (search engine software) to move around and find your content, feeding that information back to the search engines.

Categories help form the structure of the website, and tags also create structure by linking posts together. You don't have to use either of these, but I use both on my blog. Take a look back at Step 2 in Chapter 3, where I've provided examples of how categories can be used on a blog.

Tags work in a similar way to hashtags on Twitter. I tend to add new ones on a regular basis, and have a widget on my home page which displays the tags in different sizes according to how often they're used (a tag cloud). This helps to add another layer of structure to the site, benefitting both search engines and viewers.

Tailoring the Text for Search Engines

I've read various pieces of advice and I'm not certain what works best, but I've stuck to these rules about text and they seem to have worked well for me:

Titles

Try to include key words in your blog post titles e.g. 'book', 'review' and the title of the book, and name of the author.

The First Paragraph

Make sure you include plenty of key words in the first paragraph of each blog post, but not in a way that sounds strange or stilted. Take a look at the first few sentences of one of my blog posts, with key search words highlighted in bold:

"I heard **Jake Arnott reading** from his **novel, The Fatal Tree,** at the **Hay Festival**, and was intrigued by his use of slang **words** – a **historical** dialect of thieves and villains, taken directly from the "flash world" of Romeville in 18th century London. The **book** centres on the true **story** of infamous jail-breaker Jack Sheppard and his companion, the notorious Edgworth Bess (aka Elizabeth Lyon), but it is not a straightforward telling."

Post Length

Try to make your posts at least 500-600 words long. Search engines seem to be more likely to pay attention to a post of this length. I find that 600 words is about right for most posts anyway – many more and the reader will stop reading, although there's nothing wrong with variety.

Search Engine Registration

Some of the advice out there suggests registering your website with search engines. This acts as a kind of invitation to ask them to visit your site and take a look, if they haven't done so already. There is also a lot of advice which suggests that this isn't necessary. I would consider looking into this and researching the various options only if you have waited a few months and still can't see any results when typing unique chunks of text into a search engine.

Images

Give images a relevant title and an 'alt' name (text alternative), and use key words, e.g. the title of the book which is in the image.

Links

If you get another, more popular, website to include a link to your blog, then that will have a really positive effect on your own SEO. One way of doing this is to add your blog to some blog listing sites such as **www.bookbloggerlist.com** although you may need to wait a few months until your blog is established to become eligible.

You can leave comments on other blogs, with a link to your own. This is common practice among book bloggers, but make sure you have something interesting to say, as well as posting your link, otherwise you're just creating spam. You could also contact the website owner and ask whether they will include a link in return for you adding a link to their site.

If an author likes your review, they may be willing to include a link on their own website directly to your blog post. It's worth being strategic when you start out, prioritising reviews of books whose authors have a website of their own, and a following on social media. If they link to your review then lots of people will see it, and that will increase your own following.

Creating Unique Text

Ensure that you don't copy whole chunks of text or entire posts from other websites. That's not good practice, but it also confuses search engines to the extent where they may blacklist your blog if they think it's not posting original content. Try to avoid other people copying your own text too.

Titles & Permalinks

Each page and post that you create will have a permalink - a unique URL e.g. **http://createdtoread.com/book-review-the-miniaturist-jessie-burton/**

As you can see from this example, the blog domain name appears first, followed by a title which WordPress has automatically created, based on the title of this particular post. With most blogs, it will be possible to change these permalinks to make them more search engine friendly.

Some blog platforms will automatically create a permalink using the date, but search engines prefer key words to numbers. That's why I usually include the words 'Book Review' in my post titles, along with the title of the book and the author's name. I sometimes delete generic words such as 'by' or 'of', but try to keep the meaning, so that it makes sense to people as well as search engines.

Chapter 5: Content Creation

Creating Pages

There's an important difference between 'pages' and 'posts'. A 'page' is static and if someone signs up to follow your blog, they won't be notified about new pages, whereas every time you create a new 'post' they will receive an email, and the most recent post will appear at the top of the list, with the older posts moving down.

I write all my posts and pages in Word before copying them into WordPress. The main reason for this is so that I can use the spellchecker, and it also means I end up with a second copy saved on my laptop, just in case.

Here are some 'pages' you may want to create:

About & Contact

Nearly every website or blog has an **About** page which gives a short introduction to the blog and explains what it's all about. You may also include contact details here, or you could set up a separate **Contact** page. Most bloggers include a photo of themselves. I'd advise getting a really good photo taken by a friend. It's worth spending time on this. Take a look at other blogs and see what they include. If you've had any writing published you can include links to it here. Try to keep your **About** page up to date, and include links to any social media accounts.

Note of caution: Remember that any information you post here will be visible to anyone, anywhere in the world. That includes your colleagues, relatives, and any potential publishers or employers, as well as total strangers. This may seem obvious, but in the excitement of blog creation it's easy to forget.

Reviewing Policy

You may not feel that you need a **Reviewing Policy** but then again you may be amazed by the number of authors who get in touch asking you to review their book. Personally, I think it makes a blog look more professional, and it helps filter the review requests. I specify particular genres that I'm interested in, and others that I don't read. If you do start getting bombarded with requests, it can be a helpful way of justifying a negative response. Don't feel obliged to review every book that you're offered. It's your blog, so you can post what you like.

I also state in my **Reviewing Policy** that sending me a free book doesn't guarantee a positive review. There have been a few books which I just didn't enjoy, and preferred not to post anything at all, rather than a negative review. You'll have to decide how to deal with this kind of thing. Balanced reviews can be interesting to read, but personally I don't enjoy reading an entirely negative review.

Privacy Policy

To be honest, I included this mainly because it makes the website look more professional. I don't currently store anyone's contact details apart from the email addresses in the RSS feed. I copied the general details of my privacy policy from another blog. If you do copy something like this from another blog, make sure you don't just copy it word for word, change it to fit your own needs.

Writing Posts (part 1) – The Book Review

Writing a book review can be relatively straightforward, but it can sometimes be a real challenge. I try to take the pressure off by reminding myself that I don't have to review every single book I read. If you can't think of anything interesting to say about it, then perhaps you need to think a bit longer, or perhaps you should just enjoy reading it and move on to the next. Don't let blogging take over your life so much that you no longer enjoy reading!

Work on more than one

When you begin writing, one thing I would recommend is that you don't just try and write one book review, and agonise over getting it right for ages and ages… Instead, work on two or even three separate reviews to begin with. See what happens; create draft posts and see how they look using your 'preview' feature. Don't put too much pressure on yourself. Working on several pieces at the same time will allow you to spend time away from each of them, and go back with a fresh perspective, able to see what works and what doesn't.

Start before you finish

I generally start writing a review whilst I'm still reading the book – often with about a quarter of the book left to go. By this point I'm fully immersed in the book's world; I make notes on the basic plot outline and the characters' names, and how they interact; I think about the themes and I bookmark particular passages that I like or which seem to sum up what the book is about. By the time I've finished writing the review, I've usually started reading the next book.

Begin well

People don't spend long reading online, and your first sentence is essential – it has to grab their attention and keep it. You can start with anything you like, but these are three good ways to begin:

- Give a short and concise summary of what the book is about in your opinion

- Provide a short summary of the plot

- Describe how you ended up reading this book (if it's an interesting story)

Here's a review which I've started in a fairly straightforward way, with a summary of my own opinion on the book, followed by a description of the plot:

"**My Falling Down House** is a philosophical portrayal of what it means to be reduced to nothing, to become a nobody, to fall to the very bottom of reality and to question what it is to be human. The book transports the reader to Tokyo and a young man named Takeo Tanaka, former employee of a company hit by the financial crisis. He loses his job, his girlfriend and his home in quick succession. Having lost everything, he moves into a frail, abandoned house, made entirely of wood and paper, and attempts a total withdrawal from society."

And here's one which starts a bit differently, with a more informal, personal take:

"This was a random find in an Oxfam bookshop in Chester – one of those buys where you look at the front cover (I must admit this didn't really draw me in), scrutinise the blurb, scan a couple of pages and you're still not absolutely sure... but it turned out to be one of the best books I've read all year, so well worth the £4 that I paid!"

Use a conversational tone

I try to write using a conversational tone, more informal than the kind of language you'd use in an academic essay or even in a magazine article. Blogs are supposed to be like diaries or journals, and I often include personal information e.g. where I read the book or what made me decide to read it.

Create a structure

My usual format is to give a concise sentence describing my opinion of the book in the first paragraph, followed by:

- A summary of the plot, which I usually write in my own words (some bloggers copy out the blurb from the back of the book but I prefer not to do that)
- Description of the themes in the book
- Discussion on what I think worked well or not so well
- Comments on characterisation, plot, language and structure
- Assessment on how engaging the book was

- How it compares to other work by the same author
- How it compares to similar books of that genre
- I try to finish with a summary paragraph, using words that can easily be turned into a good quote.

Vary your language

I try to make sure that I don't use the same tired old phrases all the time. The word 'gripping' is a great way to describe a good book, but if you use it in every review your readers will soon stop reading. Try to find different ways to say the same thing. "I couldn't put it down" or "The suspense continued right up until the last page" are different ways of saying the same thing. Use a thesaurus if you get stuck.

Ratings

I don't use ratings on my blog but many book bloggers do. It's pretty difficult to rate books against each other, especially when they're different genres, but readers do tend to like that kind of thing. I have a 'highly recommended' tag which I try to use sparingly. If you do want to rate your books, you'll need to decide how to display the rating on your blog. You could create images, or there might be a plug-in you could use. You'll also need to decide how to rate them. Here are some examples I've seen on other book blogs:

- From 1 to 5 stars
- A rating out of 10
- Using categories such as 'Not bad', 'OK', 'Good' or 'Exceptional'

If you're stuck...

Only when I get really stuck or particularly confused about a book do I search online for other reviews. This can be helpful if you're confused about the plot, or unsure about a subtle reference to another work of literature. Then I will use them only as a way to kick-start my own thought process. I always make sure not to steal phrases or sentences. There'd be no point in doing that – I enjoy writing my own reviews, not copying other people's reviews.

If you're still unsure about your review, I would advise saving it and forgetting about it for a few days. Some reviews take longer than others, and when you look back at what you've written you may find it easy to add the finishing touches.

Adding links

I often include a link to the author's or the publisher's website, in case people want to purchase the book after reading the review. It's a good way of supporting the industry. It's useful to include links wherever they make sense, such as links to other posts on your own blog, or links to other books by the same author. You could also include affiliate links, if you want to make money (see page 58).

Include an Image

Try to add an image for each blog post. Most bloggers simply use the cover image of the book, which is often available online, but I prefer to take a photo of the book. Try to develop a consistent way of displaying images, as it makes the blog look more professional. I would recommend Microsoft Picture Manager for cropping, re-sizing and altering images (it can be installed on later versions of Office) but there are many programmes you could use.

Make sure you save all your image files in a logical place as you may need access to them at a later date e.g. when advertising the post on social media.

An example

Here's an example of a book review. Have a look at the first paragraph. I have tried to include a few key words such as the title of the book, and the words 'novels', 'read' and 'story'. I've also summarised the plot, but without giving anything away. Does this first paragraph make you want to continue reading?

"Time's Echo is one of the most gripping novels I've read in a long time. It follows the story of Grace Trewe, who is staying in York to settle the affairs of her late godmother (Lucy) who drowned in mysterious circumstances. Grace is a keen traveller, fully intending to move on once the house has been sold, but memories of surviving the Boxing Day tsunami still haunt her, and she soon begins to have nightmares of drowning. These strange dreams, which appear to be set in sixteenth century York, seem frighteningly real, until past and present begin to merge into something quite extraordinary..."

This first paragraph is followed by two more, which continue to summarise the plot in a way that provides just enough information to capture your attention, without revealing what actually happens. Together, these first three paragraphs act as a kind of extended blurb – just that little bit longer and more detailed than what you'd get on the back of the book. But it's also completely subjective – I've given my own opinion here, and that may well be different to what other people think.

In the fourth paragraph (below) I begin to reflect on the book as a whole:

"The plot is complex, and I found it almost impossible to put this book down. The lives of these two young women seem to become more and more entwined, as Grace confuses her attraction towards Drew with Hawise's relationship to her husband; and her dislike of the charming young Ash, with Hawise's fear and hatred of Francis. It seems that the past is trying to teach her a lesson, but she is confused and afraid, aware that her godmother may have re-lived Hawise's life as well, and inexplicably afraid of the River Ouse."

This continues with further discussion on the style of writing...

"There is a strong focus on tangible details, from the scent of cloves and rotting apples to the heavy skirts and linen cap worn by Hawise. It is also fascinating to see the city of York through the eyes of someone in the present, who is able to see what was once there, the layers of time overlapping in the street names and buildings. The book makes you examine your own life too, touching on family relationships and the effects of trauma.

I was afraid that the ending would disappoint, but the suspense continues right up until the last moment, when Grace realises that she must face her own fears to save someone she cares for, and, in doing so, puts her own life in danger. It's historical fiction at its best – real and frightening, vivid and acute."

These final paragraphs examine the themes of the novel, summarising my overall opinion of the book. I have created my own form of suspense in the review by touching briefly on sinister details such as the protagonist's fear of the river, leaving this open-ended and unexplained.

I've also finished the review with a concise summing up of what is good about this particular book, in a sentence that will be easy to use on social media in the form of a quote:

"historical fiction at its best – real and frightening, vivid and acute".

Publishers and authors really like these 'quote' phrases. They cover their books in them, and you may find them quoting yours, and linking to your review if it's particularly good.

Read the full review here - **http://createdtoread.com/book-review-times-echo-pamela-hartshorne/**

Writing Posts (part 2) – Other Types of Posts

Readers like variety, and I often vary my posts to include interviews, listings or reviews of events. Here are some suggestions:

How To Write An Interview Post

Interviews can be very simple, but they can also take up a lot of time and effort. You can interview someone in person, by phone or in writing. I've interviewed people both in person (time-consuming but you get a much more 'genuine' sounding piece) and in writing, though never by phone. Here are a few suggestions for how to go about it:

Research the interviewee

Do some research first and check whether there are existing interviews already online. You don't want to simply repeat the same information. If someone has already been interviewed several times, try and come up with something that will make your interview stand out, and ask different questions.

Prepare your questions in advance

If interviewing in person, I find it easier to have the questions writtern on a separate sheet of paper and to number them so, when I'm taking notes, I can just write the relevant number and concentrate on listening to what the person says.

Don't rely on recording equipment

If you're interviewing someone in person (or by phone) you can record the interview (make sure you ask first). But don't rely on your recording equipment. The first time I tried recording an interview it lasted nearly 3 hours (that's longer than most!) and I hadn't pressed 'record' properly, so I had to rely on my handwritten notes.

Remember that you are the editor

When you're looking through the questions and answers, remember that you can remove things (e.g. where the person has said something twice, or something that doesn't quite make sense, or if they have used a swear word). You can also change the order of the questions, so long as it doesn't change the meaning of what was said, as this may help give the post a better overall structure.

Here's an example of a good structure for an interview:

- Begin with a question about the writer's background, how they ended up writing their book and what inspired them.

- Move on to ask more specific details about their work e.g. how they came up with a particular character, or how they developed their plot.

- Finish with a question about what they're working on at the moment, e.g. the novel they are currently writing.

Include plenty of photographs

Interviews often tend to end up much longer than book reviews, so I usually try and include relevant and interesting photos every two or three paragraphs, to keep the reader interested. Ask the interviewee to provide photos, and include images of their book covers or photos of the books too.

Check your facts

There are two ways to do this. You can send the entire finished draft to the interviewee to check for any miss-spellings or misunderstandings, but they could send it back with hundreds of corrections, especially if they're a writer!

Alternatively, you could pick out any facts or spellings you are unsure about, and ask them to double check these, which means you do run the risk of missing other potential errors. I've tried both these methods, and I'd say it depends on the interview and the interviewee. If in any doubt, get the whole thing checked before it goes live.

See examples of interviews on my blog:

An Interview with Mab Jones - This one was conducted in person, with me taking notes, and ended up being very long.

http://createdtoread.com/from-stage-to-page-interview-poet-mab-jones/

An Interview with David Thorpe - This one was conducted via email.

http://createdtoread.com/climate-change-fiction-celtic-legends-interview-david-thorpe/

How To Write A Feature

If you want a bit of variety on your blog, try and include some features. The trick is to come up with something that your readers will find helpful or inspiring, or something which collates information or links from other websites, which they won't find anywhere else. I've written features on a wide variety of topics.

Here's a link to a feature about Roald Dahl: http://createdtoread.com/roald-dahl-storytellers-legacy/

The Guest Post

Guest Posts are useful in many ways. You can contact a fellow blogger and ask if they'd mind you writing a guest post on their blog, which will help you to reach out to a new audience and also gain a link to your blog on another website. They're also useful on your own blog to add a bit of variety and help fill in gaps when you're extra busy.

The Listings / Recommendations Post

Listings are posts which include a list of links to other websites, usually in the form of recommendations. They can be very popular, but they often require a lot of work and maintenance. I have created a few of these on my blog, including one which lists useful websites for finding information about literary events and festivals - http://createdtoread.com/top-5-sites-uk-literary-festivals/

The Image Post / Event Review

It's worth bearing in mind that you don't always need to write a lot to make a post worth reading. Although it's good (for SEO) to include at least 500 or 600 words of text, the human reader can equally be satisfied with a series of photos and short snippets of interesting information. This works particularly well for an event review. It could also work well for documenting some kind of trip e.g. to see the home of Jane Austen, or a series of photos capturing the highlights of a book tour.

Chapter 6: Some Useful Tips

Storing Your Files

When you begin a book blog, it's a good idea to plan where you'll store all your files. The blog itself will be stored on the server of your host site, whether this was free or one that you have paid for. Try to get a back-up option. It may be included in the cost if you paid for hosting.

It's a good idea to create a good filing system for any drafts or images too. I write nearly all my posts into a Word document before copying them onto the blog. I actually have a separate image folder which I regularly go back to, as I re-use the images again and again on social media. It's also a good idea to back-up these things, just in case. I am not very good at this, but it's useful to build backing-up into your weekly routine.

Statistics & Popular Posts

You may be able to view statistics directly or via your hosting site. I use a plugin called Jetpack which I find quite helpful to see which posts are more popular. It's also really useful to see how people are arriving at your blog, and to compare your monthly viewing figures.

Twitter can sometimes give the impression of being very successful, if you tweet about a new blog post and get 20 retweets. But if you look at the statistics, you may find that only three people actually clicked on the link and visited your blog. I've noticed that Facebook is often more effective than Twitter at bringing traffic to my blog.

Making Money From Your Blog

This is not my area of expertise, but there are plenty of books and blogs which focus entirely on how to make money from blogging. Here are five suggestions to consider, if this is something that interests you.

1) Basic Advertising

Once you've developed a decent amount of interesting content, and have some subscribers and a following on social media, it is worth considering advertising. People tend to find adverts irritating and it's important to think about how this will affect the look and design of your blog. You can be minimal with adverts, but the income will also be minimal.

Anyone can sign up to Google Ad Sense (or a similar system), and it takes just a few days to find out whether you've been approved or not. If you do want to give this a go, search online first for some advice about how to get approved e.g. you may need to add a privacy policy to your site, as this can help.

2) Affiliate Links

These are much more lucrative but more time consuming to organise. They work in a similar way to adverts, but you gain commission if people actually end up making a purchase by clicking on your link. Amazon has an affiliate scheme, but other booksellers such as Waterstones have them too.

Here's a post which gives advice about using affiliate links on your blog: https://ablogonblogging.com/how-to-add-use-affiliate-links-on-your-blog/

3) Selling Products

If you can write a book, produce a downloadable resource or create an online course, then you will be able to sell it through your website. This is an indirect way of making money from your blog, but once you have a platform, and regular visitors, it can be an effective tool for marketing your own products.

4) Paid Reviews

Some companies will pay for you to attend an event or training course and post a review of it. I know this can work well with other types of blogs. It is also possible to get free entry to an event in return for a review, just as it's possible to get a free book. It's always worth asking – you never know.

5) Donations

It's fairly easy to set up a PayPal account and then you can create a 'donations' button for your blog. You are providing a service (interesting / useful content) and some people may be willing to donate a small amount of money if they feel they have benefitted from it.

Being Flexible & Responding To Trends

I started by posting twice a week, on Tuesdays (to make use of #TuesdayBookBlog) and Fridays (to make use of #FridayReads) but soon noticed that Fridays (and weekends in general) were not very popular for blog visitors. I decided to try posting on Thursdays instead of Fridays, and this has had a positive impact on the number of views. Since then I have had some periods when I've had less time to commit to blogging, and so I've gone down to just one post a week, sometimes less.

I also write regularly about literary events, and sometimes try to post my review immediately after the event, or the following day - the more immediate the post, the more relevant it is, and the more likely it is to be picked up on social media. It's important to be flexible and to make the most of opportunities that come along.

The People Behind The Books

When I first started blogging, I was shocked to discover that authors responded to my reviews! That may sound naïve but it's easy to forget that books are written by real people who might read book blogs. Writers can be sensitive people, and if you are commenting on their book then you need to remember that they can read your comments, and so can their friends and family. If you want to include negative comments, be cautious and fair. Bear in mind that even a seemingly positive comment could be read the wrong way by someone who is hyper-sensitive about their own work.

On the other hand, it's important to be honest. If you don't like something about the book, that's fine, but try to balance this alongside more positive comments. People read book blogs for honest recommendations, where they can get more details than they would from simply reading the blurb.

Security, Passwords & Problems

When you begin to create your book blog, you may well register for several different accounts on a variety of websites and social media platforms, ending up with multiple usernames and passwords which you will never remember. It is a golden rule never to write down your passwords, but this was the only way I could remember them all, so I would recommend choosing a safe place and keeping a record. It's also good policy to change your passwords regularly, and to ensure that you don't use the same passwords on different sites.

Every time you log in to your blog dashboard, you will see comments and notices. It's important to log in regularly (daily if possible) to keep an eye on things. Many bloggers recommend updating plug-ins as soon as they alert you to the fact that there's a new update available, and checking your comments regularly to approve or respond. You may get a lot of spam comments, and there are plug-ins which can help sift through the spam, such as Akismet.

How To Get Free Books

If you're keen to get your hands on new books it's not that difficult to get hold of free review copies. One method is to use listing sites such as **www.netgalley.com** where you can register yourself as a reviewer and request books. I haven't used this method as it's rather unpredictable and there are a lot of reviewers competing for a small number of copies.

Personally, I don't enjoy reading novels in electronic format, but if you're happy to read e-books then they are often much easier to get hold of, or cheaper if you end up buying them.

Most publishers will have a named contact person listed on their website for marketing and reviews. Once you've established your blog, and posted a few reviews, it's worth emailing these people directly with a friendly request, explaining why you're interested in a particular book. Include a link in your email to an example of one of your best reviews, and some statistics (e.g. how many views you get each month). Begin with small, local publishers, who will be keen to get a review from anyone, and give them your address so they can post the book straight away.

There's also the library, of course, and you may be able to request books, even if they're not in your local branch, or you can also borrow books from friends.

Pleasing Your Book Friends

It is excellent advice to say that you should never review books by people you know, especially good friends, as this can get complicated. You will want to give them a good review, but this could put your honesty and integrity into question.

However, this is easier said than done. In reality, the book world is small, and you may find that you quickly become friends with those whose books you've reviewed, as well as publishers and booksellers. My rule, which I am trying to stick by, is that I will reserve judgement on a book until I've read it. I won't promise a review, until I am certain that I can write a good one, and that it will be as fair and unbiased as possible.

If I don't review a book, it's not necessarily because I didn't enjoy it. It may simply be that I'm busy or tired, or can't come up with a good summary. It may even be due to my lack of knowledge in a particular area. I've made decisions not to review books which have been incredible, simply because I didn't feel able to do justice to the quality of the work.

It's also useful to remember that there are alternatives. If your friend has written a book, but you don't feel able to review it, then you could interview them instead, or ask them to write a guest post about their inspiration, writing process or experience of publication.

Re-sizing Images

It's important to ensure that your images are not too big (otherwise they may hamper the loading speed) or too small (so they don't look blurry). They will appear different on different devices, but I find that if you go for a maximum of about 900x900 pixels, and a minimum of around 600x600 pixels, they are usually OK (these are the figures for square images but hopefully it will give you an idea).

I use Microsoft Picture Manager to edit images. If you want to use it in a recent version of Microsoft Office (2013 or 2016) you'll have to download it, as it's no longer included – follow these instructions online: **https://www.howtogeek.com/281913/how-to-bring-back-the-microsoft-office-picture-manager-in-office-2013-or-2016/**

In Microsoft Picture Manager you can just click on 'Picture' and 'Resize' to change the image size easily.

Formatting Sideways Photos

There is a problem that can occur when using digital images, where the image appears sideways on some devices, and in some programmes, but appears upright in others. This caused me major headaches when I first started blogging, partly because it can be unpredictable. I had to quickly remove one or two images from my blog, after it had gone live. Fortunately I don't think many people had noticed.

It's important to keep track of how your blog looks on different devices. If you don't own a smartphone or iPad, ask a friend to check how it looks on theirs. Images won't always be lined up the same way, but most themes are now mobile friendly, so they should work well on whatever size screen you are looking at.

The sideways photo issue may not be a problem for you, but if it is, the best way to prevent it is to make sure you remove all properties from a photo before adding it to your blog. Right click on the image, then click on 'properties'. You may need to switch to the 'details' tab, and then you should see an option to 'remove properties and personal information'. This should remove any hidden instructions from the camera or phone which was used to take the photo.

If you're still having problems, another very simple method is to paste the image into a PowerPoint slide, turn it around and edit it exactly how you want it, then save the slide as a .jpg image itself.

The Virtual Blog Tour & Book Giveaways

These are two promotion strategies used by authors to connect with readers, boost sales and increase their audience, and they are often used simultaneously. They are more commonly used for genre based e-books such as YA and Romance.

Virtual Blog Tours often take place over a few weeks. Several book bloggers take it in turns to run features on a new book, often in the form of a review, a guest post from the author or an interview. This can be daily or weekly, or less structured over a month or so. The author benefits by reaching a new audience via each blog, and the bloggers benefit too, gaining interesting content and often increasing their own audience.

Some authors will organise their own blog tour or 'giveaway', while others may get help from their publisher, or they may pay for a service from a specialist company. Virtual blog tour websites will have a list of blogs that they regularly work with, and you could easily sign up to one of these, although it helps if you've already built up an audience and can prove it with some statistics.

Here is one example of a blog tour website, where you can sign up to take part: **http://tlcbooktours.com/be-a-tour-host/**. If this is something you're interested in, search online for 'Book Blog Tours' to get an idea of how they work, and whether this is something you'd like to do.

Giveaways can take place at any time, but they seem to be most effective when co-ordinated with other techniques, and boosted by assistance from other social media users. I've never organised a giveaway, but they can be a useful way to gain followers, subscribers or Facebook page 'likes'. They're probably best done in co-ordination with the publisher and author, to get maximum interest.

Problems With Formatting

When pasting text directly into your blog from Word or another programme, you can encounter problems such as extra spaces appearing, or different line breaks. This can be an issue particularly if you're quoting a poem or similar piece of text, where the formatting is important.

The problem can often be solved by editing the text in 'text' or 'code' view (where you can see the code version of the blog post). In WordPress, you can easily switch between 'visual' and 'text' view, and compare the two. You don't need to know a lot about computer code to be able to make simple formatting changes, and if you're really stuck you can often find the answer to a question by searching online.

Take a look at the following example, where I've pasted some text into a blog post, and extra spaces have appeared in between the lines, which seem to be stuck there. Then look at the next image, which shows the 'text' view of the same piece of text. By removing the lines in 'text' view, they disappear in 'visual' view (you can see the two tabs in the top right corner).

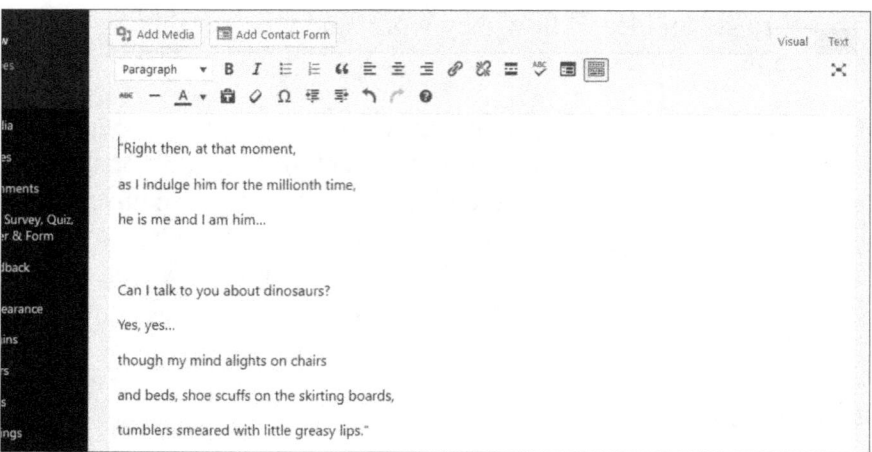

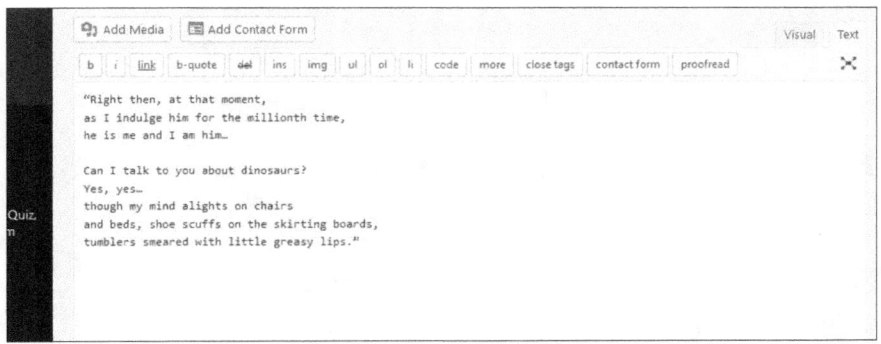

There is a lot more that can be done with code, but you may find that your particular theme will limit what you can do with formatting.

Your First Review

If you've found this book useful, then please do have a go at writing a review of it. Even if it's only a few words on Amazon, they'll do their bit to help others make a decision as to whether this book might be helpful. Perhaps it will be your very first review!

About The Author

Rachel Carney started her blog in early 2016. Since then she has written articles and reviews for several magazines and websites including the Welsh Agenda Magazine, Wales Arts Review, The Poetry School and the New Welsh Review blog.

She is also a poet, and runs a monthly writing group at her local arts centre. Visit her blog **http://createdtoread.com/** to find out more.